Angelic Whispers

Susan Williams

Angelic Whispers

Copyright © Susan Williams 2004

ISBN: 1 903607 59 0

All rights reserved. No part of this publication may be reproduced, stored in a retrieval system, or transmitted in any form or by any means, electronic, mechanical, photocopying, recording or otherwise without the prior written permission of the author.

Typesetting and Production by

Able Publishing
13 Station Road
Knebworth
Hertfordshire
SG3 6AP

Tel: 01438 814316 / 812320
Fax: 01438 815232
email: books@ablepublishing.co.uk

www.ablepublishing.co.uk

Acknowledgements

To my Mum and Dad

Thank you for the love and security you have given to me throughout my life. Always know you hold a special place in my heart.

To my children Martin, Donna, Matthew, Claire and Kirsty

We have had a few rough rides along the way but together we have made it. Know I am so very proud of you all, each unique in your own way, but not one more special than another.

To my friend Frances Boyd

A true ambassador and teacher for Spirit. Without your guidance and your love this book would never have been. Thank you for picking me up each time I fell and for believing in me. Know my love travels with you, always.

Foreword

For about eight years now I have been walking a spiritual path.

I lost my son to leukaemia in 1978 and for such a long, long time I was lost, not knowing where to go or where to look for answers to my questions, always wondering if in some way I could have prevented this terrible tragedy. Although I always had the support and love of my parents and family, there was always an emptiness that I could not fill and a knowing within me, that there had to be more than this earthly life we live.

For many years I went through the motions of living, bringing up my family and trying to make some sense of all that had happened.

About five years ago I found myself at the local Spiritualist Church, looking for answers and I have to say hoping to be reunited with my son in some way.

From that first visit I knew I had found a way of life that could take me places I would never have imagined, open my heart to things I could only dream of and introduce me to people who to this day enrich my life and have taught me the meaning of unconditional love.

These past few years meditation has become a part of my life, and to anyone who has not tried this, I would say make it part of your daily life. To sit in the quietness, still your mind and give yourself time to connect with just who and what you are, can truly make you feel a calmer, happier person, more in control of your life than you have ever been and knowing that with patience and practise there may be a chance that you too could connect not only to your higher self but perhaps those in the realms of Spirit also.

About a year ago I felt the need to have pen and paper by my side during my daily meditation time. I didn't understand why, I just knew that it had to be.

One day as I sat, I had words in my head that I knew were not my thoughts and I picked up my pen and wrote word for word what was being given to me. At the time they had no meaning but later as I reread and typed them up I was amazed at the clarity and meaning the words had.

At first I thought that I had written them myself, but after trying unsuccessfully to recreate them and also being told "No offence, but you are not that clever!!!" I accepted the fact that the two worlds were joining for a brief time here and there to communicate with each other. I could not work without them and they could not work without me.

I shared the words with people around me and it was only because of their reaction that I realised what a gift I had been given. Since that first day I have been lucky enough to receive many such words from my friends of the spirit world.

They have always asked that I share them with as many people as I can and this I have always tried to do with my circle of friends and acquaintances. Some have been read out at the Spiritualist Church where I have now been a member for many years. More recently I have been brave enough to actually stand up and read them myself and although it filled me with terror I have to say that it also gave me enormous satisfaction to be standing passing on the word of spirit to so many.

Always in the back of my mind had been how could I reach more people, a few friends had been telling me I should publish them. Hence the idea of the book was born.

I hope that the messages and words of wisdom that follow will give to you the enjoyment and upliftment that I received while writing them.

If just one person is helped by these words then I think the aim of spirit will have been achieved.

Susan xx

Dedication

My son, Nicki

Your earthly life was but a few short years but during that time you brought happiness and laughter into so many lives.

The sorrow and the pain will never leave me but because of your passing I have learnt many, many lessons. I have been able to help others when they have been in need because of my own experience. I have also learnt that no matter what life throws at one there is goodness and happiness to be had from any situation.

Had you not gone on along your pathway, I would never be where I am now, and believe me son it is a good place to be and I thank you.

You have given me strength, you have given me determination. You have given me friendships so strong and so good that I know I shall never be lonely again. You have opened up a world to me that in my ignorance I never knew existed.

So today Nicki, I dedicate this book to you and I celebrate your life, a life that is everlasting, for you have not gone, you are so close some days I could reach out and touch you. If I could but see your heavenly form I could hug you and smother you with kisses just the way it used to be.

I do not weep any more. I think, I remember, I smile, I laugh and I thank God that he brought you into my world, even if it was for just a short time.

I will hold you in my heart forever.

Angel Lad

I have a little angel
He lived here once with me
I know he comes here often
I can feel him, just can't see.

His heart's no longer beating
I know his pain is gone
He has moved across the threshold
The soul I know lives on.

I know I cannot keep him
I know he must go on
But I also know he's near me
That he never will be gone.

So if you do not need him
For a minute here and there
Could you send him down to me Lord
I will keep him in my care

When my mind is quiet and empty
With silence all around
He can come and sit beside me
And converse without a sound

We could sit and have a chat then
We could hug the Angel way
We could just be one together
For a moment in each day

The years have come and gone now
The time keeps moving by
But our love will last forever
We are bonded him and I

I know one day I'll see him
I'll look around and there he'll be
What a moment to be treasured
What a wondrous sight to see

For now I have my memories
Of the time we've had to share
But if he needs me, ever needs me
Just you tell him, I'll be there

For the worlds they are together
I know they intertwine
For I can step in his world
And he can step in mine

My heart he'll hold forever
My love will always be
His to have and keep Lord
For all eternity

Healing For Mother Earth

Hello my friends, we are glad you come together,
There is not one amongst you who is not important,

We need to ask of you, your help,
The vibrations are changing and so must you all,
The earth needs healing, great healing, we weep,
Man has no idea of his damage,
The torment he causes his earth.

Send it love, not in a big way, but as you go about your earthly day,
Take a moment to give thanks for all around you,
Healing For Mother Earth
Wish it well and send it love,
Many help but more are needed,
This planet needs kind words and love, just as we,
Send forth your love as you walk with your world,
Give it your blessings, let it know you care,
Heed these words as man cannot live forever unless they do.

Many try to help this planet, but many more are needed,
Listen and you will be guided, watch and you will see,
Love this earth, spare one thought for its beauty each and every day,
Work with us for it's survival,
Be not afraid to try, this world of yours need healing.

We can help but the toil must be yours,
Such a gift to you, It needs your love,
Be wise my children, do not forget the most precious gift of all,
Heal it now.

We are wise, we have knowledge, but you must be the instruments,
We endeavour to guide but will you listen,
We think so,

Go forward, a thought each day, a caring gesture is all your world needs,
Be at one with your world, give it continuous life.

We are not here to preach,
We are here to help,
Always.

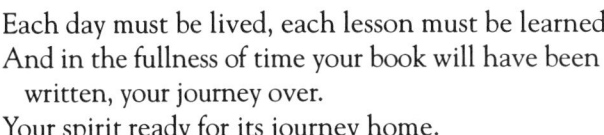

Look into yourself to see where you should be going
No one can tell you, only yourself
A journey filled with lessons and experiences
Maybe not the journey that you intended but one that must
  be fulfilled.

Each day must be lived, each lesson must be learned
And in the fullness of time your book will have been
  written, your journey over.
Your spirit ready for its journey home.

Along your pathway kindred spirits will cross but also others who will test
  you
and put upon your path obstacles to be overcome
These are the true lessons that you have decided you must learn
Do not turn from them, go forth and find wisdom
Once learnt this lesson shall not cross your pathway again.

You will find your answers in the strangest of places
Perhaps from people and spirits that you in your human form would
  rather not be acquainted with
Trust the inner you, go with the inner faith
Open your arms to all who draw near in your lifetime
And learn to see them as they truly are

Discard the shell and look for the inner beauty
Sometimes this will be hard but in the knowing,
you will find contentment often and understanding.

Life's lessons are unfolded in the strangest of ways.
But all you will ever need to complete your journey will be placed upon
your pathway
Learn life's lessons well
Experience all that is given to you
Experiences of joy, love, pain, fear and wonderment are all yours
Take them, rejoice in them and fulfil that in you that must be fulfilled
You are you, be true to yourself and live in a way that you can believe in
We are all different, unique in many ways
But the inner you will be your guide to know that you are living in truth

Walk with pride, walk with love and tenderness
and know that you will never be alone in your
hours of need
The love of spirit surrounds us all

Enjoy your journey
Travel with care
But fulfil each footstep

Fear

Fear comes from within, it manifests inside our very being.
It eats away at our very core.
To live in fear is not to live it is to exist.
It manifests and allows us no peace.
Fear knows no boundaries.
It eats away, takes hold of your thoughts.

Living in fear is like a time bomb ticking away making each day a day when you wonder if indeed you can survive it.
It crawls over you, stops you dead in your tracks when you least expect it.
It grips at you so tight you wonder if you can ever loosen its grip and move forward.
It rears its ugly head any time, any place, having no regard for your thought, feelings and well being.
Never asking are you ready, are you brave enough, have you the inner strength to do battle with this something you cannot see.
Your heart cries out no, but inside you already know that you have no choice.
You must live the fear, breathe the fear, and trust that you will come through.
To survive you must confront it
You must live, breathe, eat, sleep it until you realise you can survive.
No matter what form your fear takes you can take hold of it, confront it and come through the other side.

It is hard to climb a mountain, each hold a struggle, each breath taken sheer agony as you battle within yourself for the courage to go on
But once you reach the summit and know that you have succeeded and survived your fear will go.

The first step is the hardest, knowing that you can take on your fear, you can battle it, and you can win.
The higher self, the real you, knows what lessons you have to learn, lean on the inner you, it is strong enough to carry you both.
Give it free reign, let it do battle, let it become the strength and courage that you need
Walk tall, walk into your fear and know that nothing is insurmountable.
Have faith and trust in yourself to realise that you are strong enough to fight and survive from the demon you know as fear.
Take a deep breath, walk into the fear, let it engulf you, you will come through, emerge triumphant knowing this fear cannot harm you again.

FEAR CANNOT SURVIVE UNLESS YOU LET IT

A World of Love and Peace

A small insignificant flame flickers in your midst. Unbeknown to all but a few.
A candle of love, a candle of hope, a candle for our tomorrow.
A tomorrow for our children, a tomorrow for our world.
A new era is coming, a new way of life is dawning.
Will you join us, will you learn?
There are but a few who have ignited this flame, but soon many flames will flicker throughout the world, bringing togetherness and love, stamping out poverty, pain and anguish.
We have sent teachers to help the many who are amongst you with the gift and knowledge to carry our words and love to your brothers and sisters throughout the world.
This will be a wondrous time, a new beginning.
A unity is being formed, a brotherhood of spirits.
The world is ready.
The knowledge is sparse, but we are here, on hand to guide.
Listen and you will hear, seek and you shall find.
The pathway is rugged, the labour and toil will be hard.
We have sheep and shepherds.
The shepherds amongst you are becoming aware of themselves as I speak.
The sheep, unbeknown to themselves at present will awaken when the time is right.
They will be guided and nurtured until they are able to see their intended passage of life.

The meek shall inherit the earth.
The unified meek will lead this world back to a place of beauty and love.

Great knowledge has been made ready for those who seek.
Pieces of a huge puzzle at present, but gradually they will interlock and be interwoven together to become a unified whole.

Those who are seeking, have faith.
Those who fear what they don't understand, turn to those that guide you, listen in faith to the words being uttered.
But a few to some but for others many more.
Those with knowledge must teach
Those looking for enlightenment must listen
Soon the listeners will become teachers and new followers will arise from the masses.
The tiny sparks of light will become huge flames burning for those who wish to follow.
A world of light, a new tomorrow.
We are awakening, the dream about to be realised.

Children of the world the time is coming to ignite your flame, the flame that burns within your being.
Give of your inner self, unify and grow strong.
Bring about the changes to your world that are needed.
Rekindle the lights that have lain dormant.
Make them shine for all the world to see.
Many will be waiting for the brightness to take them out of darkness.
Show them the way and they will follow.

Unite and live as spirit intended, it is time to make your world a place of beauty and of love.
Have faith in each other, make it your world.

Oh how bright your light will shine.
A beacon of love, light and unity.

On that day the dream of many will be fulfilled.

A Christmas Message

I am a messenger of Spirit

I have glad tidings of great joy
Man has begun to love his brother
No gift could be more welcome
This season of goodwill at last begins to have meaning
The true gift of Christmas comes from within, the gift of love.
The gift of sharing, the gift of togetherness
Lift up your eyes, look around, see what man has done to man
And start at this special time of year to change the way of man
Embrace your brother, bring him into your life and let him share in your gladness and your sorrow.
The greatest miracle of all was not the birth of one man, but it will be the birth of a true nation, great, yet humble enough to know that the greatest gift of all that can be given is love.
That one man, the Christ child showed you what is possible if you would only choose to follow in his footsteps and give of yourselves selflessly to your fellow man.

The way of your world at this time of year is of materialistic gifts, to show you are thinking of others.
This is your earthly way we understand this.
But the greatest gift of all is free, but much harder to give, the gift of Self.
Embrace each other, a hug, a smile, a word of kindness
How many faces can be lit up just by a meeting of eyes, the mirrors of our soul.
Hold out a hand to a fellow man who may be stumbling along life's path, finding it a wearisome journey
Perhaps more so at this time of year

Peace on earth, goodwill to all men.
To all men.
Let us work to make this the true gift of Christmas

Emanate the Christ child
Become a beacon of light to all around you who have need of your love
Let them know you care, let them see the way forward
The way to give and love and understand the needs of all around them
Give of yourself the way you would want them to give
Caress and enfold them in loving arms that can only make them see
 what a gift we hold within us, if only we are able to open up and share
 with all those we encounter along life's pathway.

This Christmas time give your earthly gifts but also give of yourself, the
 greatest gift that one man can give to another

The Gift of Love

Do not be afraid, the great spirit holds us all in his arms of love, he will
 not let us fall and stumble
To give is to recieve, to love is to be loved
What power you all hold within your hands if you but knew it
The gift of love, the greatest gift ever given

Enjoy this season of goodwill
We send you our love, we ask nothing in return
Only that you open up your hearts and express the love you have within
 in any way that you can to those around you

Remember the gift of Love is the greatest gift of all

Blessings to you all

What is Faith

It is believing what you cannot see,
Accepting the unknown for just what it is,
Something that you probably will never understand,
Following blindly, not seeing, but truly knowing you will get where you
   need to be,
It is a knowing that you are never alone, nor ever will be,
At times it waivers and you falter on your pathway,
You feel that you will be deserted for not having the courage or trust to
   let go and believe in that which you know to be there but cannot see.

Sit quietly, close your eyes,
Forget the sense of sight and work with the others,
What can you feel, what can you smell, what can you touch and hear?
Close your eyes, step into the unknown,
Be guided by what you feel and touch and smell, knowing you will never
   be misguided, never deserted, always being given what is right for you,
   at that time, in that place, to fulfil the need within you.

It is good to question, but don't let go to that which is in front of you on
   a whim,
To come this far and forsake that which you have been looking for would
   not only be a waste of time and effort,
That which you are seeking may go so far from your grasp you will never
   see the true wonderment that the soul can achieve,
Is it so hard to trust that which is always around you,
Whispering in your ear, pushing you where you need to go,
Placing you in the path of those you need at that moment in your life.

We will not forsake you, we will not leave you bereft of that which is so
   rightfully yours to have,
Have courage, have faith, have belief in the one true thing that will
   always prevail,
The Love of Spirit.

Even now you doubt what you have been given,
Is it me? Is it them?
We work together, one cannot work without the other,
Rejoice in what you have been given,
And know it comes with our love and blessings.

Self Love

"I am at one with myself"

The words everyone would love to utter and truly mean
To look upon oneself with joy and contentment
So hard to do but why?
Are you worthy of self love?
How do you earn it, Where do you find it?
You cannot find it, it is not given
It is within each and everyone of you

Start your own crusade, find and conquer this little thing inside you that says you are not worthy
Everyone is worthy
You were born out of love
You were given from spirit out of love
And now is the time to love oneself
The loving of oneself is so important for mankind
To go forward in a world of peace
We must create love and peace within
To teach others to find the inner beauty we must first obtain it for ourselves
How many of you can say it is felt by you, for you
So many of your tomorrows depend on the love that you have within

A person who has found love in their own heart for themselves owns a powerful emotion,
A powerful weapon that can be used to conquer that which is happening in your world today
To find this love, first you must go within and find the stillness in your heart
Then smile and say to the inner you , " I love you just the way you are, for the person that you are"
Worry not how others see you, they are unimportant
Instil in your self, self love doesn't have to be earned , it is a gift, rightfully yours
Something that has always been yours and will remain so

At this time it is hard for you to accept these words
They feel wrong and undeserved
They sit uneasy within your being
This is not something we can teach you
We can only ask you to be kind to yourself
Give to yourself the way you are willing to give to others
Remember you are also worthy of your love

So pure an essence, so great a vibration
When you truly find it your heart will sing
and you will weep, tears of joy
The feeling that you will have within will be one to treasure - forever.

The Children - Our Future

Many things have been forgotten
Many ways and customs that were followed
Hidden in the yesterdays of our people

This world is one of chaos
Fear, anger, greed fuels many lives
Forgotten are the ways of oneness
Forgotten are the truths each one of us hold within us
Mankind are heading for disaster, disaster of their own making
Some cannot be helped, some will not be helped
And others are here to learn lessons, hard lessons, they will not change

This must not stop you
Others can be saved by love, forgiveness, understanding
It must come from those of you that are strong enough and willing to try
Do not deny yourselves the chance to learn
It is in the giving that we receive

There are teachers amongst you all who can make them listen
Who can hit the right chord in their hearts and make them aware of the beauty that surrounds them
The fight is not lost until the battle is over
There are those amongst you strong enough, determined enough to turn many from the pathway leading nowhere

They are our tomorrow
Do not fear them, pity them, help them towards their rightful path of tomorrow
They are more frightened of themselves than you are of them
Without the anger they have nothing

The alternative ways must be taught gently but firmly, starting now
By all who have the faith and courage to do so
It can be overcome
Do not turn your back on all that has been achieved
They will not win unless you let them
They will not change unless you lead them, the answers are within you all

You are all responsible
One Father unites us, the same spirit lives within us all
Mankind must live as one, unify and make it happen.

A New Beginning

Greetings my friends, we join you once again
To prepare the way for a new beginning
Time for man to be committed to mankind is near
To give with out question and ask nothing for oneself in return
We ask that you look within yourselves now
Prepare yourselves for what lies ahead
A new dawn, a new age, a new tomorrow.

A time for man to lead man, to unite in brotherhood
And make steps towards a oneness of souls
To give without question, to liberate a freedom that can be shared by all.
To live in love and trust that for many years has been lost along the wayside
Humanity is caring, it has just forgotten how
Man in his wisdom has changed the values of life
Forgetting the true ideals that were created at the beginning of time.

Guidance is around you, opening souls that have been dormant
Listen to your hearts and give of yourselves
Your lives will be truly enriched, the tomorrows of time will be joyous
The love of man returning to where it once was

This new era we have coming will have many changes brought about by man
So that they may once again live in harmony
No more can be said at this time
Prepare yourselves for a brighter tomorrow

So many words can be given to you that you have heard before
But unless they are seeds within your heart, we cannot put them there
Now is the time to look inside yourself and see what is truly there
Each man in the quietness of his time

Higher Self

A oneness with all around you
A knowingness of all that is within you
Sit within the quietness of time, link with the part of you that is your true being
Bring forth your inner wisdom and your inner knowledge
It is a place of beauty and serenity
A place that is there for you to attain when you are ready
A place shall we say where your two minds meet
A place where one mind can ask and the other mind can answer
We are all part of the great spirit
Therefore the answers you receive from your higher self will always be for the goodness of your soul

Whatever answers you are searching for are within you
Go deep within yourself
Learn the art of listening without hearing, learn the art of feeling without touching
The beauty of the higher self is that it is always with you wherever you go
Awaiting your call to re-unite and be at one with your earthly soul
Perhaps for just a brief moment or perhaps a while longer

Let your mind grow and walk within you
Let it reach out to the hidden knowledge within you
The knowledge that you have carried with you since the beginning of your journey
We will guide, but remember we are as one
The higher self is but a part of you that is waiting to be rediscovered by yourself
Be truly at one with yourself
Open your heart, open your mind
Trust in your own ability to unite and be at one within yourself, you are part of the great divine spirit of love

You hold the key to your own learning
Believe, trust and go within
Your true power awaits you
That which we call the Higher Self

Who Are You?

You are who you say you are
You are who you want to be
Not a reflection of another
A true being, a spirit of light
Become who you are, wonder at nothing
Fulfil that which is within you and enjoy the journey
Be not afraid of what or who you are
Rise up like the eagle and take flight
Welcome your experiences, embrace your passions and accept the you
    that you are
Feel the pains, the joys, the caresses and the love
Life is given
How you express it lies within you
A lifetime is but the blink of an eye, time is nothing
Experiences will be many, observe them well
Do not make judgements, observe, learn and teach, give and take
One can never know what lies ahead
Just accept
For with acceptance comes abandonment to fulfil even more of that
    which you have come to express
The tides of life are many, but with each one will come fulfilment
Catch each one and ride upon the waves of life
Journey into the unknown, you can never fail
This can only be if you do not venture forth, to fail is not to try
Walk forward in the knowledge that you are in charge of your destiny

The hopes and dreams that are within you are all reachable, if you will
   allow yourself the freedom of the spirit that is within you
Never be afraid it will not happen, be more afraid that, the truth in the
   living will far outweigh the dream in the heart
Have courage, have faith and have belief in yourself
The trueness of your being will not fail you
The soul within you has such a passion for life
Allow it to be, allow it to break free and fly
Give it life and see where you travel
Give it expression and it will create
Your tomorrows are in safe hands
They belong to you.

Spring Awakening

The echoes of the stillness are nearly over
All that has lain dormant is awakening
Mother Earths slumbers are over
As she awakens to surround us with her love
   and beauty once again
Let us awaken with her
Let us see the beauty that surrounds us all
Hold this splendour within your heart and let it sing within you
Teach the children of your world, the beauty of her
Teach them to respect and love that which is irreplaceable
The beauty that surrounds you is for all to love and cherish
Grow in knowledge and understand the reason for her being
Blend and become one, compliment each other and understand the
   energies you share
Wonder at the creations which unfold at this time of year
The wonders of mother nature astound you still
Re-creation, it happens like a miracle

We ask you to share the beauty of your world but also the responsibility of her care and keeping
If all is to remain as it has for many years
It is important that you hear her call for help
Hear her murmurings asking for all to love and cherish from the smallest bud to the mightiest oak
Treat your earth with care , give healing and love
How can you repay mother earth for her splendour and beauty?
Simple, treat her as your equal, give her respect and love
Look for her needs and grant them, they are simple and few
Treat her with care.
Walk quietly, her whisperings can be heard if you attune yourself, converse with her and she will blossom
That which is taken for granted will not survive
That which is nurtured and understood will be forever

Our blessings are sent to Mother Earth

Enjoy her awakening

What Is A Thought

Never underestimate the power of thought
It is powerful
It can turn dreams to realities
It can bestow upon you many things
It is through thought that ideas are born
It is through thought that we begin to understand where our way is in this world
It is through thought that we connect with that which we cannot see
And talk to those we cannot hear
Thought is a gift that is never really used for all that it was intended

It is the thought that begins the happenings
It is the thought that makes new beginnings
Never dismiss that which comes to mind
Thoughts are you, communicating to you
Listen to your thoughts and make them realities
Turn them into words and help them breath
Turn them into words and give them creation
A single thought can change a happening
Many thoughts can change so much more
Never dismiss that which is given to you
It is always important
If not to you then another will find true meaning from it
Speak your thoughts and watch them grow
They will fulfil not only you but those around you
They will help others grow
You do not have to control
Just give the thought, let it be added to their own
And soon all thoughts will become words and words will become creation
New ways, new meanings, new beliefs
Fulfilment, contentment and happiness
Oh , so much to be given from one thought
It is strange, the simpleness of something is often overlooked
The power behind something sometimes never seen
Those that truly listen to their thoughts will find their meaning

But a few words have been given today
However they may be the most important ones ever received
Thoughts are never empty, they are full of meaning for all

They are your rememberings
They are knowledge

They are you.

Spiritual Love

Spiritual Love is a union of mind and body without even the briefest of touch being needed
It is a joyous and wondrous thing that few people ever experience and sometimes even when they do it is not recognised
It holds a rare beauty of it's own, the tender moments belong to the soul not the physical body
It calls to the higher self and gives you remembrance of the love that awaits you when you return from whence you came
It is a meeting of two small parts of the whole
The soul meets a passion equal to it's own and it knows no boundaries, holds no fear
It is a calling of two souls to unite, be one, for just the briefest of moments or for a timeless age
Do not question it's strength or reason
Just know that it is
It is within the reach of us all, none more so than another
If it caresses your heart bid it to enter
It is a powerful thing but cannot harm
Do not try to own it, just accept it's presence
Do not try to change it, let it be
Spiritual love can be all the colours in a rainbow
Can have the strength to withstand the might of many
Or can be gentle and soft, awakening slowly and remaining forever within
It can be a sharing of love without the union of the body
Whatever way it touches you, know that it is real
It is a passion of the souls
It is a loving of the minds
It is an awakening of the inner being
It truly is a union of the spirit

To whoever whispered these words in my ear – I thank you

The Souls Dream

Peace is the stillness of the soul
It is the oneness of the being
A oneness with the self, the joy of contentment
Within that peace we find ourselves
The true being, the inner light
The soul is part of that oneness
Let it free, knowing that it can never be apart from the true being of eternity
Find the peace, find the stillness, find the serenity
Within the stillness hold a vision that is you, trust the great spirit to guide you
Let your spirit free to find your passion of life
The beauty of life will be unfolded before you
Giving you the knowing that all is well
Your peace belongs to you
Your soul is the foundation of your temple
Go within, deep within and find that which you are seeking
The essence of your being will guide you
It is there in the peace
The souls dream awaits you

Truth

Truth is something very few people own
To live in truth is many peoples dream, but fewer peoples reality
Honesty with ones own soul is the first step of discovery
Compassion and understanding for ones true being are needed
One must know there are no rights or wrongs
Only understanding, learning and just being

One must learn to forgive oneself and live in the truth that belongs to them
We must own who and what we are and know it is alright just to be whomever we are
Walk with the truth in your heart and you walk with God
Walk with the truth in your eyes and you walk with mankind in love and honesty
For they will see the truth within you and know they to can unite their truth with yours
A mind of illusion is a false mind
A heart of doubt and deception is not an honest heart
A soul filled with inbred despair is so heavy it can never hope to be one with eternity
Find your truths from within and live them
It is your honesty with yourself that will plant the seed of truth
Find your truths from within and be them
It is your love for you that will bring them forth
You cannot run, your truth is a knowing, an inner knowing of yourself
It is your trust in yourself that will allow it to be expressed
Find the truth that is you and give to those around you that which you truly are
A being of love, a being of beauty, a being of wisdom and light
But most of all give them the truth
Give them YOU

Wisdom

Does wisdom belong to those who have lived to a great age?
Is it only for the wise and all seeing?
No, it is for all mankind to have, accept and grow into.
Wisdom comes to those who listen, those who search, those who have great thirst to understand and grow.

It is for all who come looking, seeking and needing a greater understanding of all that is around them and all that is within them.

Each of you has wisdom, some may say wise words, from your moment of creation.

Share them with one another, listen to that which is said around you, listen to another's knowledge and take in the understanding, which is right for you at this moment of your time.

Give your words to one another, give your learning's to one another.

This is how wisdom grows, not from very wise beings, for you are all very wise, you must just learn to share your great wisdom with one another.

All the great things that God intended to be shared cannot be bought but must be freely given, enriching many lives as it is passed one to another, bringing fulfilment and joy to both giver and receiver.

We ask of you all this day, share just one moment, one learning, one experience with another and see how the wisdom of many changes.

If mankind is going to live as was intended at the beginning, it is only by uniting in all ways that this will come to be.

Put a seed, put a thought, put a question, in just one mind each day and mankind will see changes.

Changes that have been waiting to happen for an age.

We can give many wise words and teachings but the true holders of wisdom are those that have the courage to share all that is within them.

We ask any who reads our words to have courage and faith in that which they believe and share it with all who will listen.

No man is more learned than his brother, each has something within them to enrich the life of another.

Let the wisdom be given

Let the wisdom be accepted

Let the wisdom be lived.

Blessings

Vision of Peace

The vision of mankind must be one of peace, the vision of mankind must be one of togetherness.
Without this vision man ceases to exist, in the fullness of time they will be no more.
The end of creation will be, it cannot remain unless it is the will of all.
Those who are indecisive will perish, those who are innocent will perish.
Those who are set on destruction will be no more but will have succeeded in bringing your world to oblivion.
It is in each man, woman and yes even child to bring about the change, through love and commitment to his fellow man.
If each lays down his weapon, whether it be made of material things, whether it be made of words or whether it be the weapon of ignorance, then and only then can mankind step forward into a world of harmony and peace.
Then and only then can there be a true brotherhood of man.
It is not only those who rise against their brother that cause this unrest and disunity of the world it is also he who takes no responsibility for that which is going on around him that is equally to blame.
Think of the power of the voice that could be heard with the unity of all those voices left idle through ignorance and fear.
There is not one so blind as he who does not wish to see.
Do not hide from that which you know must be done.
We would ask each and everyone of you to seek within yourselves to find what you truly wish your world to become
If it is to be a world of peace and understanding, with all man living together in harmony and love then find the courage to speak your truth.
Tell your fellow man what you expect from him, also tell him that which you will no longer tolerate
If each man, woman and child are true to their belief and add their voice to the growing number who crave a unified world then it will become a reality.
If no man picks up and throws that stone into the pool of water, the ripples in the water will not emerge and go forth to create a tidal wave of destruction

Tranquillity and calmness will prevail.
Each voice will be heard, each voice will make a difference and together you will succeed.
Violence, hatred and destruction can never and will never triumph.
Love will always overcome in the end if it is sent forth from a heart of truth.
It is your world, we cannot save it.
This lies within the power of you all.
Walk forward one step at a time, determined not to let this destruction through your wall of love and it shall not break through.
Slowly and steadily make the hatred retreat, it is like a mighty fire, it cannot survive if you do not give it the fuel with which to grow
Unite in love, unite in peace.
The greatest weapon you possess is the one of love, use it well.
Go forth and reclaim your world, then proclaim it a world of peace.

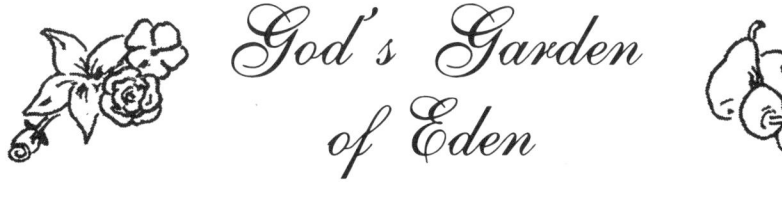

God's Garden of Eden

When you awaken tomorrow look at the world through new eyes.
See the beauty that is around you in all things.
Be at one with your world and count the many blessings that surround you.
Your world is a beautiful place in which to live.
You are surrounded by great beauty, but so often it is taken for granted.
The miracle of all you survey is not recognised for just what it is.
Do you never wonder how each aspect of your nature kingdom knows just when to come into fruition.
How each flower knows just when to bloom, how each ear of corn knows just when it is time to be harvested.
This miracle of nature is just that, GOD'S MIRACLE.
Given to mankind to enjoy, given to mankind to nurture and maintain.
We ask over the coming weeks as all the earth is in the glory of growth that you take the time to truly look around you.

At the beauty of the colours and fragrances that are so abundant at this time.
We would then ask that you give thanks for all that you have.
We ask you to be at one with your nature kingdom and as you walk through your world, be aware if its magnificence.
Spend a few moments each day, in the quietness, sending out love and healing for that which is taken so much for granted.
This world will only prosper and remain a place of great beauty if mankind nurtures that which it has been given.
With thought and understanding it will remain forever God's Garden of Eden.

Life Is Eternal

It is no shorter or longer for any of God's children
It is with faith and understanding that you will learn the truth of this
It is with acceptance that the fear within is quietened
When it is time to move on, there will be no fear, only enlightenment
As the soul ventures forth there will be no pain, only love
Know this to be true.
When near to what you call physical death, do you truly see torment and trouble, or in those last few moments of a loved ones "life", have you glimpsed the peace and serenity, which is present.
When a passing happens it is for the highest good of the soul, the spirit within is ready to continue on its journey of evolution.
Rejoice for that which is being experienced.
If you could but see how the released spirit rejoices in its freedom there would be a happiness within you all.
If you could see the glory of the angels gathered, the magnificence of their presence your hearts would sing with gladness, you would bear no sorrow, there would be no room for grief.

Think of it not as a passing, but as a passing on, a passing on to something more wonderful.

In your world there are many sayings echoed amongst you, "A gathering of the souls, moving on to pastures new, going home, even heaven", if you but knew the truth in those words there would be no longing for a soul to remain.

We ask of you all that, at a time of passing, be happy, rejoice in the life that moves on, give thanks for the time shared, the experiences gained and the memories made.

It is natural that you should weep, bear pain, sorrow, anger, resentment, but perhaps with thought in your quietness you will see these feelings are for yourselves, perhaps a small spark within remembers that from whence you came, the Kingdom of God.

Live your faith, trust your faith and know with each passing comes a rejoicing, a welcoming, as souls once parted unite once again.

When you are saying farewell to a loved one, smile, give thanks for that which has been.

Look forward to the next meeting of your souls, for it will surely come to be, as you go forward to the realms of spirit.

If you pray this night, truly pray from the depths of your being.

Ask the Great Spirit to do that, which is right, for the soul for which your words are spoken.

It will take great courage, it will take a soul full of unconditional love, it will take all the unselfishness you possess.

Think quietly before you join your thoughts to God's, for it is far harder to utter words in prayer that are truly right for another.

We know what we ask shall be hard for many, as it can be in times of great pain that your prayers are uttered, but all the strength you need is within each and everyone of you.

Remember always, LIFE IS ETERNAL.

The Journey of the Soul

The journey of the soul is a lonely one.
Touched here and there by a passing soul.
The true vision of the soul is to walk a united pathway and to give.
For to give is to receive, to share is to partake.
It is to find a destiny that unites mankind in harmony and togetherness, giving what is needed and, receiving in the fullness of time that which it is seeking.
A soul cannot be cheated out of it's learning for it will return time and again in it's quest for knowledge and fulfilment, whether there be pain or pleasure.
The soul, the centre of the being, craves many things, passion, understanding, learning, togetherness, but more than anything it has a yearning for love, both the giving and receiving.
If man has belief within himself that the journey he is taking is for the awakening of his soul, for the growth, understanding and wisdom that is needed for the advancement of his soul at this given time, then his earthly life will indeed take him to places unknown and allow him to partake in things that will not only let the soul know greater knowledge, but will also allow the soul to become something so wonderful, it can only be dreamt of in this earthly life.
As you walk life's pathway be true to that which is within you.
Allow yourself the freedom to feel all that is intended, great sorrows and great joys, the peace and the torment, but above all allow it to feel love.
So many times you are told you will not be given that which you are unable to bear. Know this to be true.
Go forward with courage.
Experience all.
Go forward and live.

What Of Love

The power of love is incredibly strong and beautiful
Nothing can survive without being nurtured and loved
The loving must start with the self and transform the inner being
It must open the inner voice to the concept that love is for all
The love from mother to child, from lover to lover
No one can survive without it
One will wither and die, if not altogether then from within
Many people touched by love do not understand it, many dismiss it and many simply choose to deny it
Is it so hard for man to realise without it one is just existing
Give of yourself but more so be open to receive
If it doesn't carry well draw it closer
The first step to living is loving
We will speak of it many times, it is the core of your being
Nothing that can be touched, nothing that can be seen
But something that can be given and received so freely and without condition
Sit quietly, go within yourself and find it's vibration, see how it resonates within your being
It is there, have no fears or worries that it shall be gone
Let it express itself within you, telling you of beauty
Let it caress you within, feel it's warmth, feel it's beauty
Feel it's overpowering strength, yet gentleness
Once it sits well within you, send it forth to touch another
No not another, many, yes send it forth to touch many
It may be fragile and weak to start
Over time with wisdom and experience, it will come to hold such passion and humility at the same time
You will give it freely, without knowing of it's strength and upliftment to another
Radiate your love, let it join with those around you
Send it forth and know it shall be received
Let the vibration of love reach every centre of every being
Set your world aglow, create a great fire of love
Make it a true universal love for all.

Two Worlds As One

We are one, the kingdom of the father is for all
We walk in unison, the two worlds side by side
Each taking from the other what is needed and understood
Look with the inner eye and you shall see
Touch with the inner being and feel
But a mere veil separates the two
There is no time only existence
The vibrations of our two worlds join closer, we walk a parallel path
In the quietness of your time we draw ever closer
The journey of enlightenment moves forever forward to a time when we will become one
The brotherhood of man will come into it's own, for we truly will become one together
Many earthly lifetimes ahead but it will happen
The spirit of man and the spirit of God joined once more in unison
One a place of celestial beauty
The other a place where the soul learns to express all that it needs in readiness to return from whence it came.
We walk in tandem
Do not hurry to be at one with spirit, just know that it will be
Feel our energy, know our love
Permit us to draw ever nearer
Vibrations are changing, man is changing
One day soon, all will know just how close we are and have always been
We will rise as one, we will be as one, as it was then, as it is now and as it will be forevermore
You are me and I am you
A creation of oneness … for eternity

The following words were written on 4th September 2004 –

I dedicate them to all who lost their lives on that fateful day.

I have been very angry today, also very sad to know that things so ugly and painful can be done by other human beings.

The words that I write now are not the ones I would have chosen to write, they were not the ones in my mind this morning as I took my anger out on my garden, trying to still my mind and my thoughts.

I sat in silence when I was able and asked of spirit one question ... WHY? Why did all those children in Russia have to die

Some people will not like the answers I received, but I must write it as it was given to me. Once again I share with you and hope that once your anger and pain subsides you will be able to see the truth in them.

Remember With Peace

Many tears will be shed today through pain
Many words spoken in anger
We ask that you forgive
The way forward is in forgiveness
You must believe in eternal life
You must believe that there was purpose to all that has happened in your world
Do not retaliate in bitterness and anger
Do not make light of the lives that were given, so that many would learn the lessons of life
There was point , there was meaning
In this moment of time still your minds , open your hearts and move your world forward
The fighting must end, the hatred must vanish
You must rejoice in the preciousness of living
Remember those that go before you with love and with pride
Now is the time for trust, now is the time for faith and belief in the inner knowing that all will be well

If lessons are learnt they will not be repeated
If man in his wisdom listens to his inner voice, the world as you know it can be one of peace
Each person must take ownership of his soul
Each one of you must take responsibility and be accountable for all that is done to those around you
Just as some have free will to let dark thoughts roam so others of you have free will to move to a new and brighter tomorrow where love and peace is in the minds and hearts of you all
To find forgiveness where there is anger, to find compassion where there is pain, shall be an insurmountable lesson for some
We ask that you see through the shadows and focus on the light
We ask that you work towards peace
Let thier silence be not in vain
It is your world, each and every one of you has free will
Join hands, open your hearts and walk forwards in peace.

May I ask each one of you who reads this to help make peace a reality. Make your voice heard, make your feelings known, join with me to make peace happen in our lifetime. Let's leave our children a world they can be safe in and proud to be a part of.

When given the following words I felt at once they had great meaning. However the title was something I pondered on for a long while.
  It was given very strongly over amd over again. Having looked it up all I kept getting was Adventis ... which does have meaning.
  I asked for the meaning of Aventis and ws told – the beginning of the new. I for one think that things are changing, I am sure others can feel it also.
  I place them in Angelic Whispers so those with a greater knowledge and understanding than myself, can interpret them as they see fit.

Coming Of Aventis

It is a rising of the souls, a fullness of the spirit
A gathering of many to begin a new tomorrow
It is a drawing close and linking of minds
It is a knowing that evolution has become
Much will be given through the minds, it is a linking of minds
Communication as is known now will have progression not to need the voice, but to need the mind
A linking of energy and vibration
A spiritual awakening
No - a releasing of the inner soul, a realisation of that which is man
Open the stillness within you, be at one with it
Prepare it well, knowing all will be as it should be

There will be a change in earth's colours, a quickening of her pulse
A transfer of physical to an elevation of awareness of the attributes of the higher being.
Let it open naturally be aware of the vibration and learn the rhythm

Aventis - The beginning of the new.

Eternity - A Passage of Time

Have no vision of time
Just open yourself to the knowing that all will be
Man has placed the time
The awakening of the heart does not come with time
It comes from the knowing and understanding that we are as one

Your seasons, they change, not by time, but in the feeling of readiness
A readiness that Mother Earth is ready to bring forth her fruits and her beauties, her Miracle of Creation
Be like her and know that when man is ready, so will his changes begin
It is coming but to prepare the whole of mankind, to awaken so many that do not as yet have the comprehension of the great plan needs much wisdom
When you are ready so shall it begin
Do not try to move mountains, go around them
Take the might from your mountains and they shall turn to dust
Surround them, find your footing and climb as one
Do not use your strength, use your unity
Cover your mountainside with love, be heard in your unity
Words spoken in silence will have far more credence than those uttered in anger
To change minds you must open hearts

The ascension of man
How long have we waited ... Eternity
But until all are ready, it cannot be
We ask patience, we ask understanding,
We ask that you let time take care of itself

Message of Love

It is simple
Learn the joy of love
Learn to give and share and be
Know that love will triumph where roads are long and hearts are heavy
Know that with the joining of souls comes enlightenment
With love comes peace

With love comes understanding
With love you view life in a way that can only bring contentment and understanding of all around you
Can we teach you love?
No - it is there within you to be awoken by oneself
Can we bring you love?
No - by giving so shall you receive it
Can you own love? - You can try, but know if you put limitations on it, it may wither and die
Give it free expression and see how the spirit soars
A small word with such power
Many say they want to find love, it cannot be found, it is already there waiting to be accepted
Waiting to be embraced and enfolded
Do not look for it, let it come to you from within
With the loving of the self, you will open your heart for the love of others to enter
Be open to receive that which is being offered
Be open to accept and cherish all that is yours to have and share
When the time is right be ready to awaken another soul to the beauty of love
Pass to another, that which you have learned is beautiful and attainable
All life is about love, the giving and receiving
Know this day you are loved
Walk forward with the knowledge and know it will forever be this way
The love of God is with every man, the love of self is with every man
Such a powerful emotion, but one that can also give peace to mind, body and spirit
Own the love within you, share it with all on your pathway
But more importantly accept the love that is given
Make your circle of life complete.

Pathway of Knowledge

The pathway of knowledge is very long and takes many lifetimes to conclude
It calls upon one to be many things
Giver, receiver, teacher, master, pupil, we are all teacher of another, pupil to someone
Who can tell where this pathway may lead
Great knowledge is attainable, but remember knowledge is many different things to many different people
With birth we learn the path of survival
With adulthood comes the knowledge of responsibility
With the opening of the mind comes the knowledge of man and his universe
No one person learns the same lessons, travels the same pathways or creates the same destiny, both for himself and those around him
No one can travel your pathway for you
One must learn to accept the lessons they are in need of and know when the pathway they are travelling has reached a crossroad
Let not another man tread your footsteps for you
Know when the time has come to walk a different path
You will be guided, you will never journey alone
All knowledge worth having has to be earned
The hardest lessons lead to rugged walkways in life, but always, without question, guidance will be given if only you open the mind and heart fully to receive
Never be afraid of what is before you, it will always be attainable, for your good and to enrich your life
Remember you are not judged, we only ask that always you give of your best
None of mankind are the same
Each is born with different lessons to be learnt
Just walk your pathway with pride, being yourself, let all other men be the master of their destiny
You are responsible for just one …

The conscience will guide, the mind will create and at the end of the day, the knowledge you have gained will take you forward into your tomorrows.

Lessons of Life

Can one survive the inner turmoil, come to terms with and understand all that is asked both spiritually and mortally?
Can peace and stillness be found within?
Does one have the depths of understanding to know why things happen and why life plans the experiences and tragedies that are given?
To be who you truly are takes great courage and strength
To understand the reason for your being you must surrender the soul in complete faith to your God, knowing he will never fail you
Can you do this?
It is hard to believe as the mortal body weeps, so the inner most part of you, the soul, grows to such dimensions
The weak and the young spirited know an easier journey, but will return
Those on a surer pathway, leading them to their vision of the Kingdom of Heaven, work for the betterment of their spiritual being
They search for the eternal spark of love that will lead them ever nearer to what is sometimes known as the "Promised Land"
The lessons of the soul can be painful, for true growth this must be so
The lesson of love is not in the physical, but is in the strength of the inner being to let go to that which is truly a part of you, in allowing the soul of another to continue it's journey is one of the greatest lessons for man
Spiritual strength and mastership comes in walking the pathway your soul has chosen, accepting all that is given, knowing it is for the advancement of the true spirit and higher self
Mortality brings limitations, with mortality comes fear.

Fear puts limitations on the learning
All man returns to the father, surrender to this knowledge and the true lessons of the spirit will begin
You shall find the strength to let those go on before you, in the knowledge that life is eternal
Perhaps this is the greatest lesson that man has to realise.
All man has within him, that which he needs to fulfil his journey
All man is surrounded by those who will guide and protect him
In the knowing that no lesson shall be to great shall you find the courage and strength to go forward
Our worlds are never far apart
Reach out a hand and we shall hold it
Open a heart and we will touch it.
By surrendering your soul you will learn the true meaning of love
Man has no better companion than his God
Trust and you shall never walk alone
Be true to that which you are
The inner being has all the strength that shall ever be needed
Trust in yourself, Trust in spirit
Together in unity
We are One

For The Love Of Spirit

The spirit within knows no boundaries in its depths of love
It will give freely to those in its path and care
The limitations of man constrict something that needs expression in many different forms
A soul, a loving soul, can transform not just the existence of it's own mortal life but those of many others.
Those who have come to know this, must realise this could be the highest lesson on their pathway

To put aside the limitations man has set and love in the way that was intended
Do not let another's misinterpretation lead to stagnation, teach them
As you misunderstood, so shall many
The unity of two souls is a wondrous thing
If this is within you then have the courage to set it free
Let not the word of man discolour something that is meant to be
Many souls join in love
It is not physical, it is the core of the being that has found a kindred spirit, that beckons fulfilment
Be reassured that with time, many of mankind will see the love of the spirit for just what it is
If not given freely the earthly body will feel its disease in many ways
A true soul will touch many on its earthly journey
The true lesson will be in the acknowledging and understanding that it is to be
The true spirit is pure, feel it's awakening, hear the beckoning of another
Have the faith and understanding to know that spiritual love is not of the body but of the soul
Many are awakening, know you are not alone
Know no fear, it is meant to be
It will unfold and touch many and with the unfoldment will come a new way of life for mankind
It is meant to be, deny it not
It is the Great Spirit, reteaching his children the true meaning of the word Love
Love is for all, to share, to give, to have
Do not give it boundaries or restrictions
Let it flow where there is need
It is time for you to lead with the intent that those around you will follow
If it has awakened in you, it is time for you to awaken another, perhaps even many
Be not afraid, give love freely and know it shall be returned
The love of the spirit has no boundaries
It embraces all.